The
Aspiring Writer's
Journal

Designed by Elisabeth Ferté
American edition cover design by Marianna Dutra
Translated by Gill Rosner

ISBN: 0-8109-7058-9

American edition published in 2006 by
Abrams Books for Young Readers, an imprint of Harry N. Abrams, Inc.

Printed and bound in China
10 9 8 7 6 5 4 3 2 1

HNA
harry n. abrams, inc.
a subsidiary of La Martinière Groupe
115 West 18th Street
New York, NY 10011
www.hnabooks.com

The Aspiring Writer's Journal

Susie Morgenstern

Illustrations by Theresa Bronn

Abrams Books for Young Readers
New York

Writing hits you like love at first sight!

That's what happened to me when I was little. Before I could walk, I was crazy about pencils and paper, any kind of paper: notebooks, writing paper, drawing paper . . . For me it was magic.

In my notebooks I could trap everything I saw and everything I felt. I could scream out loud without making a sound. I could turn a lifeless sheet of paper into a laugh. I could tell my darkest secrets without revealing them to a soul. I had company even though I was all alone. Sometimes I even managed to make the ink cry my tears . . .

Most important of all, it was paper that finally let me talk! I lived in a very noisy family, and the only way for me to get a word in was to write it down. Writing made me feel powerful. I could make my enemies disappear and create an ideal world. Writing truly is magic!

I want to share this magic with you, so I'll tell you a secret: if you want to be a writer, you have to write. Of course, that means you have to want to write! Sometimes you can be helped into WANTING something. I want to give you a gentle push, just a nudge into writing. It's something I've dreamt of doing for a long time, because I think the more writers, the merrier!

Writing is like playing a sport; you have to practice. You have to train, improve your stamina, and keep at it. You have to write every day, free up your hand, build up your self-confidence, and dive in head first. This diary will help you write something every single day of the year. In the end, it will become a habit, and you will sail along, at ease in the sea of words.

For writing and me it was love at first sight, but there are other ways. You can get there just by spending time with pencil and paper. People go soccer-crazy from kicking a ball around; it's the same for a pencil—only use your fingers, not your feet!

Once you have the urge, you can reach the moon!

So let's get started!

Susie Morgenstern

Write ten wishes for the new year.

What could be more exciting than the first day of a brand new year?
You have a whole year in front of you, and you only live once! Now's the time to take stock and make resolutions. It's the time to wonder: What do I really want out of life?

"The only joy in the world is to begin."

Cesare Pavese

January 2ⁿᵈ

"You need not leave your room. Remain sitting at your table and listen. You need not even listen, simply wait, just learn to become quiet, and still, and solitary.

The world will freely offer itself to you to be unmasked. It has no choice; it will roll in ecstasy at your feet."

Franz Kafka

People often ask me:
"But how do you find your ideas?"
This is both easy and hard to answer. My inspiration comes from life—simple, everyday life. The idea for a book might spring from something someone says, from a chance encounter with the most ordinary or extraordinary person, or just from a situation. Inspiration is often a mystery. It rushes out, just like that, without our knowing how or why. Only Kafka knew the answer to that!

Dear Aspiring Writer,

Where do your ideas come from?

Jot down four words without thinking, and bring them to life in a story.

> "You can't wait for inspiration. You have to go after it with a club."
>
> **Jack London**

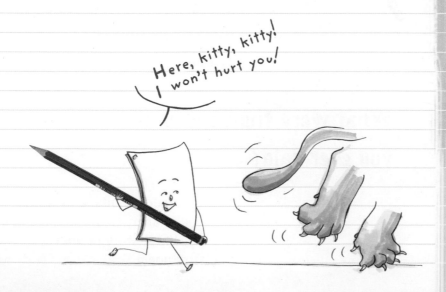

What were the first words you ever said?

"Writing is like carrying a fetus."
Edna O'Brien

Ask your parents, and while you're at it, find out if they kept your first story or your first poem . . .

Write down a sentence.
Rewrite it five times!

Either write the same thing in different ways (examples 1, 2, and 3), or add new ideas. You might even want to play around with the words and how they sound.

1. She got up, thinking that something would finally happen.
2. That morning she felt the air buzzing as if a new day had really begun.
3. That day, all at once, she felt her life was definitely about to change.

"I turn sentences around. That's my life. I write a sentence and then I turn it around. Then I look at it and I turn it around again. Then I have lunch. Then I come back in and write another sentence. Then I have tea and turn the new sentence around . . ."

Philip Roth

January 6th

"Human speech is a cracked cauldron on which we knock out tunes for dancing bears when we wish to conjure pity from the stars."

Gustave Flaubert

Rewrite the quotation from Flaubert in your own words.

"Imagination is the secret and marrow of civilization."
Henry Ward Beecher

Invent titles for three detective stories, using the following words: an ax, the moon, a gold tooth.

"When Sleeping Beauty wakes up, she is almost fifty years old."

Maxine Kumin

Make up a story beginning with this quotation.

What would you like never to end?

By the way, you're not allowed to answer "life"! It's more a question of listing your favorite moments in everyday life.

"One is never afraid of the unknown; one is afraid of the known coming to an end."
Krishnamurti

*"A comic book
is like the cinema,
even if it is
a cinema
for the poor."*

Hugo Pratt

Read a comic book and enjoy yourself.

Poor old me!
I simply can't read comics.

They make me dizzy.
I can't manage to read the text
AND the pictures at the same time.
I admire people who have this double talent.
They get twice as much pleasure.
The more you enjoy, the more you live.

So don't be like me!

Lie in bed all day, listening to your favorite songs over and over.

"Don't work too hard. Fool around a bit. Be lazy. Don't worry. Life is forever."

Henry Miller

What do you think your life will be like when you are older?

Who will you be?
What job will you have?
What sort of person will you be?
Describe your future family.

I am me!

I am you!

"It takes courage to grow up and become who you really are."

e.e. cummings

*"I say yes
and always
yes whenever
the distant,
unknown,
and beloved
beckon me."*

Khalil Gibran

Say "yes" to chocolate,
say "yes" to opening the shutters in the morning,
say "yes" to traveling,
say "yes" to friendship...

Take out your pencils and crayons, and use them to bring to life any of the words below:

Love,

Friendship,

Sorrow,

Violence . . .

"The aim of art is to give life form."

Proverb

"Life is either a daring adventure or nothing."

Helen Keller

Today,
declare your love!

January 16th

"The first poems I knew were nursery rhymes..."

Dylan Thomas

Try to remember a nursery rhyme, a poem, or a song that you often heard when you were little.

Note down the words in your diary.

> *"Any story told twice is fiction."*
>
> **Grace Paley**

Try out your talent as a critic!
How observant are you?

Get your parents to write separate accounts of how they met. Can you see any differences in the way they write . . . or in the story they tell?

Tell the story of something terrible that happened to you, or to someone you know.

"All suffering is bearable if it is seen as part of a story."

Isak Dinesen

*"If people knew
how hard
I worked to gain
my mastery,
it wouldn't seem
so wonderful
at all."*

Michelangelo

How long does it take you to write a book?

What time do we put into this crazy equation?
The nights we spent tossing and turning in bed?
The walking and stalking and plotting our mission?
The years of our childhood with dreams in our head?
The days we watched people at bus stops and stations?
The questions we ask, like what, where, how, and who?
The moments of failure, the congratulations?
The times we spent wondering just what to do?
The roads to nowhere that lead
to confusion?
The smiles and the laughs, or the
trouble and strife?
Now everything points toward
just one conclusion:
To write a good book,
it takes a whole life.

> *"My models will be forgotten but my characters are immortal."*
>
> **Honoré de Balzac**

GRANDMA! GRANDPA!

Immortalize something or somebody you love: your old teddy bear, your grandmother, your favorite aunt or uncle . . .

Write a story that you like and get a friend to read it.
What does your friend think?

Then write another story that you think your friend will like, although you don't necessarily like it yourself. What does your friend think this time?

"Write something to suit yourself and many people will like it; write something to suit everybody and scarcely anyone will care for it."

Jesse Stuart

"When making your choices in life, do not neglect to live."

Samuel Johnson

What does this quotation mean to you?

"We come from our childhood just as we come from our native land."

Antoine de Saint-Exupéry

If you have not yet read it, read *The Little Prince* by Antoine de Saint-Exupéry. Did you know that it is one of the most widely translated books in the world?

Choose something that you have had since you were little, and let it tell the story of a happy event it witnessed in your childhood.

Have you ever done anything you were ashamed of?

Write your "confession."

"Writing is not necessarily something to be ashamed of, but do it in private and wash your hands afterwards."

Robert Heinlein

"It is never too late to be what you might have been."

George Eliot

What does it take to become a writer?

Two things: you have to want to write and know how to write...
You all know how to write, and even if you don't think so,
you all have something to say. But of course, you have to want to say it!
For example, I have no particular wish to climb mountains,
but I'm sure that if I trained really hard, and if I really wanted to, I
could . . . Well, maybe only small mountains!

Here is my advice for people who ask me how to become a writer:

> A teacher needs qualifications,
> a pilot must know aviation,
> a lawyer is sure to have learnt all the law,
> and a doctor needs skill with his patients.
>
> These jobs are for experts, you see,
> but an expert you don't have to be.
> You can drop out of school
> for there's no golden rule
> saying writers need their GED.
>
> But going to school is the way
> to learn thinking and wisdom, so stay!
> For the more that you know, the more it will show
> in the great book that you'll write one day.

*"Go, not knowing where;
bring, not knowing what;
the path is long,
the way unknown;
the hero knows not
how to arrive there
by himself."*

Russian fairy tale

In your opinion,
what are you doing here on earth?

Which writer would you like to meet?

And what would you ask him or her?

Write a scathing portrait of a friend who has betrayed you!

You could also plunge into one of my favorite books, *The Chocolate War* by Robert Cormier, and find out how persecution can lead to revolt.

Explain what "school" is to a child about to start kindergarten.

January 29th

"Say all you have to say in the fewest possible words, or your reader will be sure to skip them; and in the plainest possible words or he will certainly misunderstand them."

John Ruskin

"If any man wish to write in a clear style, let him be first clear in his thoughts; and if any would write in a noble style, let him first possess a noble soul."

Johann Wolfgang von Goethe

Do you want to be president?
Write your campaign speech.

We never know where life is leading,
we do not know where we will end,
we do not know where we'll be dwelling,
or who'll come along as our friend.

Small surprises and happenstances
springing up across our path,
some dark as night, some bright as day.
After long experience
we see it has to be that way.

Where would you like to go?

*"I've been
nowhere, I've met
no one, I've done
nothing."*

**Sylvia
Townsend Warner**

February

Make a list of common objects and transform them.

A table is not a table.
A chair is not a chair.
A table is a tent.
A chair becomes a boat.
A window turns into a television . . .

"We must learn to see the world anew."
Albert Einstein

February 2nd

You are accused of doing something you didn't do.
Write an argument proving your innocence.

You are suspected of
stealing from a bag
in the classroom.
The principal summons
you to his office.
How will you prove that
you are innocent?

— Farewell!
Nobody understands me!

"Loneliness does not come from having no people about one, but from being unable to communicate the things that seem important to oneself."

Carl Jung

February 3rd

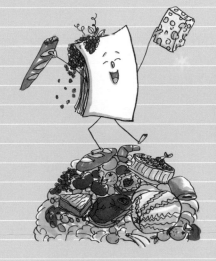

♪ Tra la la
I'm rich! I'm rich!

Use this
page to copy
out your
favorite
song.

"If more of us valued food and cheer and song above hoarded gold, it would be a merrier world."

J.R.R. Tolkien

February 4th

You are a journalist in charge
of an investigation . . .

Investigate your grandparents or any elderly people you know.
Find out what they are still curious about,
what they would still like to do,
and what still amazes them.

"I am not young enough to know everything."

J. M. Barrie

Pick a blade of grass and try to write about its awesome and mysterious side . . .

Will you be my wife?

"The moment one gives close attention to anything, even a blade of grass, it becomes a mysterious, awesome, indescribably magnificent world in itself."

Henry Miller

February 6th

Think of a road you know well.

What associations does it have for you? How does it make you feel?

"There is a road from the eye to the heart that does not go through the intellect."
G.K. Chesterton

Use this page to write down your doubts and everything you are unsure of.

February 7th

I'm not sure . . .
I'm not sure . . .
I'm not sure . . .
I'm not sure . . .
I'm not sure . . .
I'm not sure . . .
I'm not sure . . .
I'm not sure . . .
I'm not sure . . .
I'm not sure . . .

"When we are not sure, we are alive."
Graham Greene

Think of something terribly sad and try to make your readers cry.

Now it's your turn to cry—but from pleasure—when you read a book that impressed me recently: *The Curious Incident of the Dog in the Night-Time* by Mark Haddon. It's about a boy who doesn't see life as other people, and when you finish the book, you will see everything differently, too.

"How can you write if you can't cry?"
Ring Lardner

How old were you when you wrote for the first time?

I started to write before I was born,
I'm sure, without a doubt,
floating alone in my dark cell
I couldn't make the smallest yell
not ready to come out.

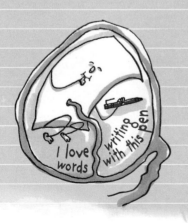

On starting school I fell in love
with my pencil—oh, what fun!
We flew through pages without bounds,
we loved to play with words and sounds,
homework was quickly done.

I'd sit up in my room for hours
and long into the night.
I'd copy a thick book or three,
lines were no punishment for me,
so much I loved to write.

"The only thing I was fit for was to be a writer, and this notion rested solely on my suspicion that I would never be fit for real work, and that writing didn't require any."

Russell Baker

What is the strangest thing
you have ever done?

Ask someone like a teacher or parent to tell the
story of what you did from their point of view.

"To write is to admit."
Kristjana Gunnars

Tell the story of a huge disappointment.

What were you hoping for at first?
What happened?
How do you see this incident now?

*"Almost all our sadnesses are moments of tension, which we feel as paralysis
because we no longer hear our astonished emotions living."*

Rainer Maria Rilke

Who are you? Start by finding out what you were like as a child. Have you changed?

"Every child is an artist. The problem is how to remain an artist once he grows up."

Pablo Picasso

You arrive in a place where nobody
speaks your language.
What happens?

"All language is a longing for home."
Rumi

For Valentine's Day, write an ad to find the love of your life. How do you see your ideal valentine?

"It is my heart that makes songs, not I."
Sara Teasdale

Choose a metaphor for life . . .
Off you go!

Life is . . .

Life is . . .

Life is . . .

Life is . . .

Life is . . .

Life is . . .

Life is . . .

Life is . . .

Life is . . .

Life is . . .

"Life is a blister on top of a tumor, and a boil on top of that!"
Sholem Aleykhem

February 16th

Starting with the first
sentence of the Bible,
"In the beginning, God created the heavens and the earth,"
tell your own story of creation.

"Adam was the only man who, when he said a good thing, knew that nobody had said it before him."

Mark Twain

Good-bye adverbs, good-bye adjectives, good-bye descriptions . . .

Take a page you have written and get rid of everything you find unnecessary!

"I believe more in the scissors than I do in the pencil."
Truman Capote

Take today off!

"Writing is easy: all you do is sit staring at the blank sheet of paper
until the drops of blood form on your forehead."

Gene Fowler

Write down the recipe of your favorite soup.

Be like a top chef: don't forget the ingredients, and invent new mixtures and taste them as you go along. When you finish, find a name for your soup! Like writing, cooking is a true act of creation.

"A first-rate soup is more creative than a second-rate painting."

Abraham Maslow

Writing helps us know who we are.

I am	yes	no
Shy		
Joyful		
Moody		
Talented		
Confident		
Kind		
......		
......		
......		
......		

"To write is to locate my own address inside my head."

E.M. Broner

When did you last say "thank you" and really mean it?

February 21st

"If the only prayer you say in your whole life is 'thank you,' that would suffice."

Master Eckart

February 22nd

What about you?
How do you escape from the truth?

Go for a walk? Block your ears?
What else do you do?

"It is good to know the truth but it is better to speak of palm trees."
Arab proverb

What would you like to be written about you when you die?

Find the obituaries page in the paper.
Then write your own obituary!

"I don't think anyone should write their autobiography until after they're dead."
Samuel Goldwyn

A day to let yourself go
and do whatever you like!

Go ahead!
Let yourself go!
Do something you've never dared to do:
dress in something weird,
talk to people you don't know,
kiss the boy or girl you dream about!
And if you really, really can't—
well then, write what you would *like* to do!

"Anyone who says sunshine brings happiness has never danced in the rain."
Anonymous

Write about your favorite playground memory.

"The world is a playground, and death is the night."
Rumi

Is everything you do absolutely necessary?

We all have rituals
and gestures that
we repeat every day.
Make a list of every
single thing you do
before you go to
school. What can you
eliminate?
Bad habits can turn
us into our own worst
enemies.

"Each soul is the hostage of its own deeds."
The Koran

What do you need to be able to write?

Raymond Queneau said:

"Take one word and then take two.
Start them cooking like a stew.
Take a pinch of common sense
and a lump of innocence.
Heat gently on a steady flame . . .
Good technique you need, of course.
Then, pour on enigma sauce.
Sprinkle with stars—it cannot fail.
Salt and pepper and . . . set sail.

Where are you trying to go from here?
To be a writer, did I hear?
A writer? Really? . . . Oh dear!"

Easy recipes

"A writer needs three things, experience, observation and imagination, any two of which, at times any one of which, can supply the lack of the others."

William Faulkner

February 28th

So that it never disappears,
write about a memory you want
to keep forever.

"What isn't written down, disappears."
Alice Munro

A day to relax—
but only if it's a leap year!

"He who seeks an easy job goes to bed exhausted."
Yiddish proverb

Make a list of the rules you live by— a sort of personal "ten commandments."

"There are three rules for writing the novel. Unfortunately, no one knows what they are."
W. Somerset Maugham

Describe an important "first" in your life.

Try to give as much detail as possible, as if you were writing this episode as the scenario for a film.

"Sing unto God a new song!"
The Bible, Psalm 33:3

Tell the story of an event
(a dinner, a game, a film) in three different ways,
depending on who is telling the story.

"In literature, there are no good or bad subjects, there are just good and bad ways of writing about a subject."
Julio Cortazar

Think of the word "computer" and write a list of all the words that come to mind.

Only stop when you have found
the word which, for you,
best corresponds to the object.
This is called "word association,"
and you can use it whenever you have
trouble finding the "right" word.

*"I follow a thread till I find something I was looking for.
When I find it, I stop."*

V. S. Naipaul

Think of an object.
Describe it to your friends without saying
what it is. Did they guess right?

"We don't see things as they are, we see things as we are."
Anaïs Nin

Write down a word,
then keep writing for ten minutes
without stopping.

This is a game to show you that the more you write, the easier it gets!
Write as fast as you can without taking the pen off the page.
Don't worry about the spelling or punctuation!

"You keep putting one blessed word after another, just as you hear them, as they come to you."

Anne Lamott

Rewrite the quotation
from Robert Burns
but only use the first and last lines!

"Ae fond kiss, and then we sever; Ae fareweel, alas, for ever!
Deep in heart-wrung tears I'll pledge thee, Warring sighs and groans I'll wage thee!
Who shall say that Fortune grieves him, While the star of hope she leaves him?
Me, nae cheerful twinkle lights me, Dark despair around benights me."

Robert Burns

Today is International Women's Day!

Compare yourself to your
mother when she was your age.
What has changed?

*"A woman who is convinced that she deserves to accept only the best
challenges herself to give the best. Then she is living phenomenally."*
Maya Angelou

Write an advertisement for any common object.

Show consumers why they can't live without it!

"The invariable mark of wisdom is to see the miraculous in the common."
Ralph Waldo Emerson

Send a letter to your imaginary French cousin, recommending three books by American authors.

Choose three books
that you absolutely loved
and try to explain why
to your cousin.

"Nobody but a reader ever became a writer. You have to read a thousand books before you can write one."

Richard Peck

Every hour during the day, try to find a word that best expresses how you are feeling.

Repeat the exercise in a week's time, and compare the results.

8 a.m.

9 a.m.

10 a.m.

11 a.m.

12 p.m.

1 p.m.

2 p.m.

3 p.m.

4 p.m.

5 p.m.

6 p.m.

7 p.m.

8 p.m.

9 p.m.

10 p.m.

"A woman is in her words."
African proverb

Choose three words at random from the previous page and use them to write a paragraph.

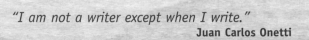

Complete the following:

I remember . . .

I don't remember . . .

I still have . . .

I've never had . . .

I see . . .

I don't see . . .

I know . . .

I don't know . . .

I want . . .

I don't want . . .

I wonder . . .

I can't stand . . .

I love . . .

I try to . . .

I don't try to . . .

"A true believer begins with herself."
Berber proverb

Page for girls . . .

What about you? Why do you want to be loved?

If you can't answer
this question
(or if you are a boy),
read a book written
by a woman!
Here are a few I'd like
to recommend because
I loved them myself.
First of all, everything
by Charlotte Brontë,
especially *Jane Eyre*.
Did you know that
Charlotte Brontë used the
pseudonym Currer Bell,
because in those days
it was a disgrace for
a woman to be an author?
Fortunately, times have
changed . . . I've also
read everything
by Jane Austen,
whose *Pride and Prejudice*
is still up-to-date!
The other day, I read
Testament to Youth by Vera
Brittain. Read it if you
want to know how
far we women have come
since the nineteenth
century.

Just little ol'me!

"What does a woman want? To be loved; neither for her cooking nor her writing, but for herself."

Madeleine Chapsal

Do you think you will stop writing one day?

Writing is like living.
We never want to stop!

Would you stop eating?
Would you stop breathing?
For writers, there is no retreat.
If you don't work, then you cannot eat.
Look at Picasso and Matisse;
they could not stop,
they did not cease.
They both lived to a ripe old age
and went on painting to the grave.
You can't switch off creative passion;
it's not just any old profession.
I hope I'll write until I die.
I hope I'm right—I tell no lie!

"Advice to writers: sometimes you just have to stop writing. Even before you begin."
Stanislaw J. Lec

Go for a walk,
hop skip and jump! Look around you,
recharge your batteries.

While you're doing it, can you think of more words for walking than Hilaire Belloc?
Take deep breaths!

"In these boots and with this staff—Two hundred leaguers and a half
Walked I, went I, paced I, tripped I,—Marched I, held I, skelped I, slipped I,
Pushed I, panted, swung and dashed I;—Picked I, forded, swam and splashed I . . ."

Hilaire Belloc

Think in green: fill your mind with this color and write down whatever comes into your head.

Go on, try!
What if all the houses, schools, cars and books were green? What if your hair were green? Would life be the same?

"Green is the color of jealousy, but it is also the color of hope."
Julia Cameron with Mark Bryan

Imagine that it's your birthday.

Ask your friends to write a story about you.

"It takes a long time to become young."
Pablo Picasso

Write a haiku.

A haiku is a Japanese poem whose form never varies.
There are always three lines with the same number of syllables, like this:

—The first line has five syllables
—The second line has seven syllables
—The third line has five syllables.

Here is a modern haiku:

"A dewy sunrise
The birds singing and dancing
On telegraph poles."

-William Wyatt

"If man is to survive, he will have learned to take a delight in the essential differences between men and between cultures. He will learn that differences in ideas and attitudes are a delight, part of life's exciting variety, not something to fear."

Gene Roddenberry

Make up the instruction leaflet to the cure for your greatest "craving."

Maybe your craving is for chocolate, sunshine, writing, doing nothing . . .

"When once the itch of literature comes over a man, nothing can cure it save scratching it with a pen."
Samuel Lover

It's the first day of spring!
Send an e-mail to all your classmates telling
them how happy you feel.

"A little Madness in the Spring is wholesome even for the King."
Emily Dickinson

I'm really torn up!

A word can have several meanings
and derivations.

Make up some good puns—become a punster!

*"When I am dead, I hope it is said,
'His sins were scarlet, but his books were read.'"*
Hilaire Belloc

How would you react if an editor refused your manuscript?

Being a writer
means accepting
the disappointment
of each rejection.
It's hard. We offer
our deepest feelings,
our hearts, our lives
on a plate;
then *wham*
they throw it back
in our faces!
It's true that not
everything
we write is good.
But all they reject
is not necessarily bad!
That's life!
As for me,
when they send back
one of my books,
I have a good cry.
Then, either I bury
my poor, dead manuscript,
or else I try
to improve it.
Sometimes I send it
to another editor,
and it is accepted!

"Try again. Fail again. Fail better."
Samuel Beckett

Use your pen to attack injustice.

It takes courage to take
sides in a discussion.
If you want an example
of a writer who took sides, you
could read *The Road to Wigan
Pier*, by George Orwell. It gives a
scathing portrait of how the poor
lived in 1930s England.
Another author who spoke
out against injustice is
Mildred Taylor, whose
Roll of Thunder, Hear My Cry
evokes the situation
of African Americans
in the United States
of America. Some other
famous examples
of courage can be found
in the speeches
of Martin Luther King Jr.,
Malcolm X, or Mahatma Gandhi.

"The dead cannot cry out for justice; it is a duty of the living to do so for them."
Lois McMaster Bujold

Will your books reveal a message?

One of my favorite verbs is "to dare"!
I like daring to say that life is worth living,
I also like "to explode" with delight,
or sometimes I have "to scream out" with fright!
Not to mention "to sprinkle" and why not "to shower"
original thoughts and ideas by the hour.
We may want "to dream" of a world without war,
"to metamorphose" life, that's what we write for!

"The writer, when he is also an artist, is someone who admits what others don't dare reveal."

Elia Kazan

If you feel like it,
write a page about burping.

A writer can't avoid subjects that are embarrassing or experiences everyone has but nobody wants to talk about. Make a list of the subjects that you would prefer not to mention.

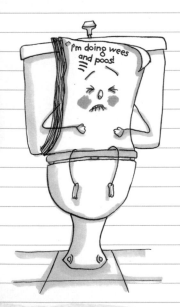

I'm doing wees and poos!

"Paper suffers everything and blushes at nothing."
Proverb

Imagine you are Rip Van Winkle
and you are fed up with sleeping!

Get under his skin: imagine how he must be feeling and what he could
be thinking about . . . Tell the story in the first person!

*"We invent nothing, truly. We borrow and we re-create. We uncover and discover.
All has been given, as the mystics say. We have only to open our eyes and hearts,
to become one with that which is."*

Henry Miller

You oversleep on a day
when you have a really
important test.
How do you react?

"To write, the first condition is to feel yourself strong and alive."
Mme. de Staël

Which of your senses
is the most important for you?

Spend the day trying to answer this question.
If you answer "taste," describe the flavor of something you ate.
If you answer "sight," describe a breathtaking landscape you saw, etc.

"Savor them in your mouth, try them on your typewriter."
Ray Bradbury

Here is a painting by Magritte. Describe it.

Ask one of your friends to do the same.
Do you see the same thing?

"The true mystery of the world is the visible, not the invisible."

Oscar Wilde

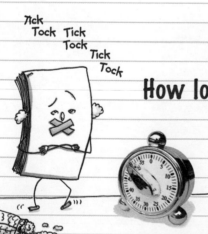

Tick
Tock Tick
Tock
Tick
Tock

How long can you stand silence?

Try to say nothing, listen to nothing, keep away from noise for as long as possible.

"The eternal silence of these infinite spaces fills me with dread."
Blaise Pascal

Go and buy a bagful of Bazooka
bubble gum, and stick your favorite jokes
from the wrappers onto this page.

Have you ever wasted your time putting in a lot of effort for nothing?

"Everything should be made as simple as possible, but not one bit simpler."
Albert Einstein

The way you dress says something about your personality. What do you like to wear?

"His clothes and ring and shoes are all going to talk..."
Anne Lamott

How about concocting a love potion?

Invent two characters, make them talk,
and make each of them like
what the other says.
Make them admire each other
so they want to see each other again.
Make them think about each
other day and night.
Make them kiss for the first time.
Make it last!

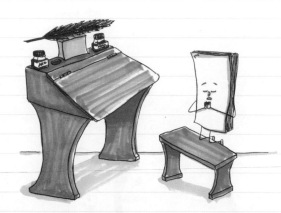

Say a prayer to the gods you believe in.

Tell them about your problems and ask them to help you.

"I have never made but one prayer to God, a very short one: 'O Lord, make my enemies ridiculous.' And God granted it."

Voltaire

A proverb is a short sentence that illustrates an element of truth about a particular situation.

Create your own proverb, using a simple truth about your life. The proverb has to reflect your own personality.

"Be not afraid of going slowly, be afraid only of standing still."
Chinese proverb

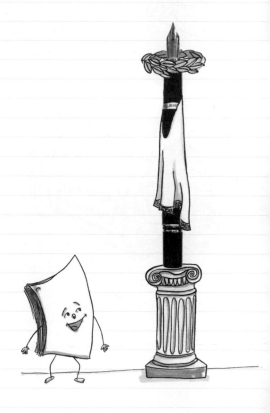

In your opinion, what does Le Clézio mean?

"Writing is the only perfect form of time."
J.M.G. Le Clézio

What are the words or expressions
that you hear most often in a day?

Which expressions do your mother, father, grandmother, brother, or best friend use most often?
What is your own "pet" expression?

"Everything has already been said; but since nobody listens, we have to keep going back and beginning all over again."
André Gide

Spend the day tracking down ideas!

Take a pencil and paper and go to different places, places you don't usually go. Inspiration will come. Seize your impressions and write down what comes into your head.

HEY!
Are you
down there?

"Ideas have come from the strangest of places."
Joyce Carol Oates

When did you last have an argument with your best friend?

What was the argument about?
What did you say?
What did your friend reply?
How did you make up?

Break me wherever you like! Look, I've got a nose and a mouth now!

"The world breaks everyone, and afterward many are strong in the broken places."
Ernest Hemingway

What if fairies really existed?

Imagine the gifts you would have liked them to bestow on you when you were born: beauty, intelligence, sense of humor, immortality, riches . . .

"When the first baby laughed for the first time, the laugh broke into a thousand pieces and they all went skipping about, and that was the beginning of fairies. And now when every new baby is born, its first laugh becomes a fairy. So there ought to be one fairy for every boy or girl."

J. M. Barrie

Which people make you want to forge ahead?

Think of the people who encourage you, those whom you admire. Then, think of people who make you feel inadequate. Think about why they should need to discourage you. Any ideas? (Reread the quotation if you're stuck!)

*"Keep away from people who try to belittle your ambitions.
Small people always do that, but the really great make you feel that
you, too, can become great."*

Mark Twain

April 13th

Spend the day making
a list of everything you don't know.

"Hopefully, I write what I don't know."
Robert Creeley

Fill in the page by completing these sentences.

I'd like to be: I am:

"To dream of the person you would like to be is to waste the person you are."
Anonymous

Today, visit a museum.

Choose a work you like and let it inspire
you to write a story.

"Art is food. You can't eat it, but it feeds you."
Manifesto of the Bread and Puppet Theatre

Boris falls in love with Alice.

Tell their story at three
different periods in history:
in 1920,
in 2000,
in 3000.

☆ CINEMA ☆

NOW SHOWING

LOVE FOREVER

NINA IN LOVE

LOVE STORY

*"There are only two or three human stories, and they go on repeating themselves
as fiercely as if they had never happened before."*

Willa Cather

Have you heard of the painter Picasso?

Go and look at some of his paintings
in books, on the Internet, or in an art gallery.
Then do what he did: close your eyes,
sing a song, and then draw something.

"To draw, you must close your eyes and sing."
Pablo Picasso

You are the mayor of your town or village, and you want to be reelected!

Write a speech outlining your plan for young people in the area. What will you do to improve school? What about sports and other leisure activities? Look for ideas and try to be convincing!

"All writing is political, because all writing is a vision of the world."
Marie Darrieussecq

Enter a competition to write about "the most beautiful place in the world"!

Describe this place in as much detail as necessary to win the first prize.

"Happily may I walk.
May it be beautiful before me.
May it be beautiful behind me.

May it be beautiful below me.
May it be beautiful all around me.
In beauty it is finished."

Navajo prayer

What makes you angry?

"Anger as soon as fed is dead
'Tis starving makes it fat."
Emily Dickinson

Do you know why
you want to be a writer?

Forever

"Writing is like getting married. One should never commit one-self until one is amazed at one's luck."

Iris Murdoch

How would you define "clean"?

Spend your day giving your room a good spring cleaning.

"After ecstasy, washday."
Zen saying

The Imprisoned Bird

Invent a biography.

Choose someone you know well and imagine his or her life from the cradle to the grave.

"The function of art is to do more than tell it like it is—it's to imagine what is possible."

bell hooks

Can you remember a situation when you were torn between two decisions?

For example, imagine you
have tickets to a concert
of your favorite band.
On that very day, your best
friend invites you to his
or her birthday party . . .
What do you do?
Write a conversation
with yourself wherein
you express your state
of mind.

Top quality!
(latest model) →

← GENUINE
quill pen

*"At work, you think of the children you have left at home. At home,
you think of the work you have left unfinished. Such a struggle is
unleashed within yourself. Your heart is rent."*

Golda Meir

Spend today eavesdropping!

Listen to conversations you hear on the bus,
in the street, at school . . .
Collect sentences and expressions people
use and write them in a notebook.
One day, you may need them to help you create
a dialogue or an imaginary situation.

*"From Mozart I learned to say important things in a
conversational way."*
George Bernard Shaw

If you want to write, the first thing to do is to get rid of your doubts: Aren't there better things to do with my life? Do I have anything important to say? Aren't there enough books already?

Years ago, my daughter Mayah put the finishing touch to the doubt I had about myself . . .

When she was little, she would tell me about her day at school. I would come down from my office with my head full of what I was writing, obsessed by problems about how my characters would react, and how I was going to thicken the plot. Mayah would talk on and on then suddenly she would look me straight in the eye and say, "Repeat what I've just said!"

Luckily, I can think and listen at the same time, and I always managed to repeat her monologue. But I know that for Mayah and for the outside world, I seemed to be completely out of it, like a sort of alien.

One day, Mayah, who had had enough of my strange ways, challenged me, "So mum, tell me what you think about when I'm talking to you!"

I told her about the latest episode of my book, and she replied with a remark that came straight from the heart: "I can't believe that a normal adult could spend time thinking about such rubbish!"

Do you ever feel bad about wanting to be a writer?

"You write and while you write you are ashamed, for everyone must think you are crazy and yet you write and you know you will be laughed at or pitied by everyone and you are not very certain and you go on writing."
Gertrude Stein

Tell the story of a day at school.

Add a few exotic touches
to your story such as
a teacher dressed
in fluorescent yellow, a friend
who starts dancing on the table in
the middle of math class . . .
Write your story with crayons
or colored pens.
Doesn't life look better
in color?

*"Make the familiar exotic, and the
exotic familiar."*
Bharati Mukherjee

Where is your favorite place to write?

Writing's a profession that can be done anywhere.
All you need is pen and paper and if possible, a chair.
You can write on a train journey while you're whizzing over land,
or sitting in a traffic jam—you only need a hand!

When you're sitting on a park bench or you're lying on the beach,
in a café, in a plane—or while your teacher is trying to teach!
You can write when lining up in shops, at least a page or two,
and in your head while walking you have time to think things through.

But for me, my house is the best place; it's where I like to write,
with my dictionaries and bookshelves and computer all in sight.
Hot or cold drinks when I want them, books and bed and telephone,
there is really nowhere better than the comfort of my home.

"It is good to have an end to journey
towards; but it is the journey that matters in the end."

Ursula K. Le Guin

Stay in bed as long as you can with a book you really like.

"Reading is to the mind what exercise is to the body."
Joseph Addison

Find a newspaper article on a subject you find interesting.

Now try to find more information about this subject.

"I was brought up to believe that the only thing worth doing was to add to the sum of accurate information in the world."

Margaret Mead

May

What would be your ideal occupation, the job you'd like to do most?

Describe as precisely as possible a day
spent working in this job.

"Being happy is a full-time job."
Pierre Perret

Read the quotation again!

How do you think writing
can save you from violence?
Write down seven sins you
think you have committed.

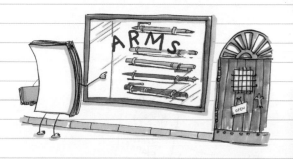

*"Writing saved me from the sin
and inconvenience of violence."*
Alice Walker

What do you expect from life?

Write a poem expressing your dearest wish.

"Life's under no obligation to give us what we expect."
Margaret Mitchell

Watch the news on TV.

Which subjects help us "understand" the times we live in?
What does the media talk about most?
War?
Poverty in the world?
Unemployment?

"History never looks like history when you are living through it."
John W. Gardner

Write a story beginning with
"You can't really be serious at __ (your age)."

"You can't really be serious at seventeen..."
Arthur Rimbaud

Do you remember a day when your shyness made you miserable? When it prevented you from doing something important, or made you feel embarrassed?

Write about your experience,
making the reader share your discomfort.

Good-bye, cruel world!

*"Being too shy to ask anyone to dance, and certain only of mixing up the steps,
I would naturally become a gibbering idiot, not knowing where to put myself."*
Honoré de Balzac

Listen to the sounds around you, and try to write them phonetically.

The sound of the sea, the wind,
a dog barking, a door slamming, etc . . .

BOING

"But if you go and ask the sea itself, what does it say? Grumble, grumble, swish, swish. It is too busy being the sea to say anything about itself."
Ursula K. Le Guin

It's bound to be a BEST-SELLER!

Do you know the secret of invisible ink?

Squeeze some lemon juice into a cup
and use a toothpick as a pen.
Then think of something you have never
dared to say and write it on glossy paper.
Put the message in an envelope and put
it aside to read later, on your birthday, for example.
Wet the paper, and your secret message will appear!

*"The pages are still blank, but there is a miraculous feeling
of the words being there, written in invisible ink and clamoring
to become visible."*

Vladimir Nabokov

In whom or what do you need to believe
to awaken enthusiasm and feel
that your life is useful?

"One needs something to believe in, something for which one can have whole-hearted enthusiasm. One needs to feel that one's life has meaning, that one is needed in this world."

Hannah Senesh

What do you do when you do nothing?

"If nothing happens, write about it."
Cicero

When what you write is sad, does it mean you're feeling blue?

When what you write is happy, does it mean you're feeling lighthearted?

"What you write is what reveals you best."
Arab proverb

You are . . .

You are . . .

You are . . .

You are . . .

You are . . .

You are . . .

You are . . .

You are . . .

It's a good friend's birthday.

Write his or her name on top of a page, then the title, "You Are . . ."
Think about the person and write down everything
about him or her that comes to mind—
a quality, a memory, an item of clothing, etc. such as:
you make me laugh, your hair's too long, you are good at math,
you lost my pen, you make good brownies . . .

"Even an idiot can be a hero . . . on his birthday!"
François Cavanna

If you could change places with anyone in the world, who would it be?

Become this person and describe a day in your life.

HEY!
Don't leave me all alone!

"There are places and moments in which one is so completely alone that one sees the world entire."
Jules Renard

You want to change something in your house (a room, a piece of furniture, an ornament . . .). How will you persuade your family?

Write a note to your parents giving your suggestions.
You never know, sometimes words are more powerful than we realize.

"One writes to make a home for oneself, on paper, in time, in others' minds."

Alfred Kazin

May 15th

What is the best memory you ever wrote about?

Oh yes!
I remember how much fun we had that day!

We don't remember every single experience in life, but certain moments stay in our heads. Writing about them is a way of reliving those moments.

"It was one of those perfect English autumnal days which occur more frequently in memory than in life."

P.D. James

This exercise is really too much! I feel ill!

Try and do what Lautréamont did: Describe yourself in the most unflattering way possible.

"I'm filthy, crawling with lice. When pigs see me, they vomit."
Lautréamont

In your opinion, for whom and what do we write?

We write for . . .

We write for . . .

We write for . . .

We write for . . .

We write for . . .

"Better to write for yourself and have no public, than to write for the public and have no self."

Cyril Connelly

The Real Me Theater

Write three portraits of yourself in the third person.
Each portrait should describe a different aspect
of your personality.

"I am he as you are he as you are me and we are all together..."
John Lennon

Do you like to meet new people?

Do you find it adds something to your life, or do you find it a terrible effort? Describe a meeting that has meant something special to you.

"I wish I'd a knowed more people, I would of loved 'em all. If I'd a knowed more, I woulda loved more."

Toni Morrison

What makes you really lose your temper?

"Eat a third and drink a third, but leave the remaining third of your stomach empty, for then, if anger overtakes you, there will be room for your rage."

The Talmud

May 21st

Turn yourself into
a lizard or a bird for a day
and describe twenty-four hours in your life.

"What can we writers learn from lizards, lift from birds?"
Ray Bradbury

Make a list of the rules that your parents have taught you.

Don't tell lies, stand up straight, keep your room tidy . . .
Which of these rules do you disagree with?

"Creative minds have always been known to survive any kind of bad training."
Anna Freud

Use this page to copy down a story you wrote that you think is pretty good, then . . . "strike it out"!

It's very hard to cross out
an immaculate sentence
that we felt to be
a stroke of genius
when we wrote it.
But the deed must be done!
Sometimes, I love a passage
in something I've written,
but deep down I know that
it weighs the story down.
So, I pick up my pen and
slash through the whole thing,
like a murderer!
Sometimes, I leave a manuscript
aside for six months or a year,
and when I look at it again,
everything that shouldn't
be there jumps out at me.
We need time to get away from
our writing and look
at it as if it had been written
by somebody else!

*"Read over your compositions and whenever you meet with
a passage which you think is particularly fine, strike it out."*
Samuel Johnson

What about men?
Don't they like clothes and scandal, too?

The quotation below is not very flattering about women, to say the least. Describe a situation where men are portrayed in a way that is equally unflattering.

"Modern women find a new scandal as becoming as a new bonnet, and air them both in the park every afternoon."

Oscar Wilde

What subject do you find the most embarrassing?

What do you avoid writing about?
Go ahead, write about it now!

Reproduction
or How
Babies
Are Made
Know-All Editions

"You must not be intimidated by your own thoughts."
Nikki Giovanni

Run yourself a bath with sea salt
(or if you prefer, bath salts!).
Stay in for half an hour. Put on soft music,
light a candle, and relax . . .

"The cure for anything is salt water—sweat, tears, or the sea."
Isak Dinesen

This is your personal Mother's Day!

Won't she be surprised!

Write a letter to your mother, listing everything she says or does that drives you crazy.
Write the truth, but don't forget your sense of humor.
Remember, only show it to her when the time is right!

"God couldn't be everywhere, so he created mothers."
Yiddish proverb

How old would you like to be at this very moment? Why?

"I can't tell you my age, it changes all the time."
Alphonse Allais

Use this page to stick all the letters and notes that you want to keep.

"Memory goes, writing stays."
Oriental proverb

The day has come for you to speak your mind . . .

So take advantage of this opportunity. If there is something annoying you, or that you have wanted to say for a while, go ahead.
But be careful: Before speaking out, prepare your arguments, rehearse your speech, and choose your moment carefully.

"Writing, like speech, is everyone's gift. Use it. What you have to say should be shouted out or written down. Let it out!"

Martin Winckler

Can you answer the question, "What is life?"

"What is life? It is the flash of a firefly in the night. It is the breath of a buffalo in the wintertime. It is the little shadow which runs across the grass and loses itself in the sunset."

Crowfoot, Blackfoot warrior

June

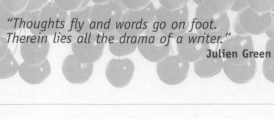

"Thoughts fly and words go on foot.
Therein lies all the drama of a writer."
Julien Green

Can you remember
a dream?
Quick, before
it flies away,
try to write
it down.

Write down memories
or pictures you associate with silence.
It's a good way to tame it.

A writer must not be afraid of silence.
He has to struggle and find enough
confidence to write his words down
on the blank page.

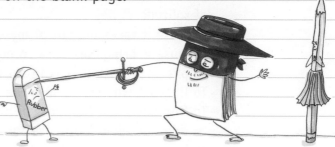

Have you ever had the impression that an author was saying exactly what was in your mind?

**That's one of the reasons I love reading so much.
Here are some others:**

- Because I'm often alone, and reading is one of the pleasures of solitude.
- Because it takes me out of myself and away from the world.
- Because it brings me back to myself and to the world.
- To put up with problems in my family and love life.
- To find out where I fit into the world around me.
- To find out the differences between men and women, and above all, to find out what life is like for a man.
- To build myself up and learn about what interests me without having to have lessons.
- To indulge in my own pleasure.
- To keep informed.
- To forget my body.
- To improve my knowledge of the world; to know what people are writing and to recommend good books to other people.
- Because I'm still looking for another Shakespeare.
- To hear people talking about human feelings in human language.
- I read because I'm human.
- To understand myself better.
- To fall in love . . . with an author, with a sentence, or with an idea.

Make up a story from
a newspaper headline.

Have you ever read a paper from last week
or last month?
It is already completely out of date and doesn't
interest us at all, because news in papers talks
about things that were only interesting when
they were written.
On the contrary, Thomas Hardy, Jane Austen,
and Charles Dickens wrote books that are
still up-to-date. In fact, no matter which era
or century, human nature doesn't really change.
Men and women have been reenacting the
same dramas since time began.
These are the stories we find in literature.

WHAT, no Dickens?

"Take care of the sense, and the sounds will take care of themselves."
Lewis Carroll

Invent a word that

sounds appealing to you.

Write it down and make up a definition.

Are you the one who took my booterees?

"Writing is an arm, a hand to touch reality. It is like trying to scratch an itch I can't reach. But it is not an itch, it is a whole world. Writing helps me be in that place where my experience is alive."
Glo Lanson

Make up a story that takes place somewhere you have always wanted to go . . .

It might be an imaginary town, a distant country, another planet . . .
You'll see––your writing will take you there!

"If I take the wings of the morning and dwell in the uttermost parts of the sea; even there shall thy hand lead me, and thy right hand shall hold me."

The Bible, Psalms 139:9–10

If you could only have one word to be your guiding light, what would you choose?

Rewrite this quotation in your own words.

June 9th

Write enthusiastically about a book you adored. You'll see that your feelings are contagious!

Hey! Move over! It's my turn now!

Brilliant book

"In oneself lies the whole world and if you know how to look and learn, then the door is there and the key is in your hand."
Krishnamurti

June 10th

Find questions that will help you to understand yourself and the world around you.

So, what was it you wanted to know?

"Writing is like palpitations of the heart, it just happens."
Elsa Triolet

Pretend you are a journalist
and write in detail about a film or a concert
that really moved you.

*"Draw a crazy picture/Write a nutty poem/
Sing a mumble-grumble song/Whistle through your comb."*

Shel Silverstein

Today, give free rein to eccentricity!
By the way, don't forget to write
something inventive!

Great!
Who says
we need cars?

"The fortunate do everything. The unfortunate have everything done to them."

Eugène Labiche

Do you think you are fortunate or unfortunate?

Explain why.

"I take a sun bath and listen to the hours, formulating and disintegrating under the pines, and smell the resiny hardihood of the high noon hours. The world is lost in a blue haze of distances and the immediate sleeps in a thin and finite sun."

Zelda Fitzgerald

Go sunbathing.

If there's no sun,
go cloudbathing.

Truth is somewhere at the center of infinity.

*Five centuries before Christ,
the great Buddhist philosopher
Prince Siddharta
set out on the roads of India
to spread his ideas.
He had a vision of the
world as a place for
compassion, meditation,
patience, and wisdom.
When he became Buddha,
he tried to fight fear
and ignorance through
his teachings.*

I dislike dogmas and absolute opinions.
Each idea has its opposite—without black, white would not exist.

I recommend you read or reread *Siddhartha* by Hermann Hesse.
It will enchant you!

"I live on good food, not on good language."
Molière

Hmm, it's a bit dry!

Make up six sentences in Molière's style.

"I live on . . . not on . . ."

You are the head
of a big advertising agency . . .

You have been asked to invent
some new warnings against smoking
to put on cigarette packs.

*"It doesn't matter who my father was;
it matters who I remember he was."*
Anne Sexton

June 18th

Write about your father.

Try to remember good times you have with him,
his favorite expressions, and your craziest moments together.

"It takes a lot of time to be a genius,
you have to sit around so much doing nothing,
really doing nothing."

Gertrude Stein

Is the time up?
Am I a genius yet?

Spend the day becoming a genius!
Do nothing, absolutely nothing!

Who are your best friends?

Stick your class photo on this page.
Write down the good and bad points
about your friends. Is anyone perfect?

"Music can make men free."
Bob Marley

Get out the pots and pans,
anything you have on hand and...
let the music play!

— Rat-a-tat-tat —

What do you find most
difficult about writing?

Sitting with the blank page in front of you, wondering
how to begin?
Finding the right words?
Being spontaneous, letting yourself go without thinking?
Reading what you have written?
Having someone else read what you have written?

When I write, what takes up all my time
is finding the plot.
What agony I go through in search
of an ending for my story!
All night I toss and turn wondering
what will happen to my characters,
who will be happy, who unhappy,
who will live and who will die.
I'm always impatient to finish a novel;
I want to know how it ends!

June 23rd

Has anyone
close to you died?

How did you feel?
What did you do?

*"The cure for boredom is curiosity.
There is no cure for curiosity."*
Dorothy Parker

GO ON, DO SOMETHING!

He's such a drag!

Begin a story with
"What a yawn . . ."

Today you are fed up with the world; you just want to sleep.
Outside the sky is gray, and life does not seem to be
as great as people say . . .

"The writer should never be ashamed of staring. There is nothing that does not require his attention."

Flannery O'Connor

Sit in a café or on a park bench.

Concentrate hard on just one person and write a description. Say what this person is wearing, what he or she is doing. Observe all his or her gestures and try to figure out his or her thoughts.

"Stop thinking and talking about it and there is nothing you will not understand."

Zen saying

Try not to think of anything
for ten seconds.
Now try twenty seconds,
then thirty . . .

"Whatever I learned, I no longer know.
The little I still know, I've guessed."

Chamfort

Make a list of everything you think there is no point in learning.

Wow! I really got all those!

Literature degree

FINE ART DIPLOMA

Certificate of excellence

"If all the year were playing holidays,
To sport would be as tedious as to work."
William Shakespeare

June 28th

Summer is
not far off!

Think of everything you'd like to do.
Describe your ideal summer.

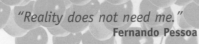

Invent a story that could have happened in reality.

Strangely enough,
I sometimes write something
completely impossible, only
to find out later that it really did happen...weird!

"Adolescence is best enjoyed without self-consciousness, but self-consciousness, unfortunately, is its leading symptom. Even when something important happens to you, even when your heart's getting crushed or exalted, even when you're absorbed in building the foundations of a personality, there come these moments when you're aware that what's happening is not the real story. Unless you actually die, the real story is still ahead of you."

Jonathan Franzen

If you had to define adolescence, what would you say?

Like Jonathan Franzen, I think adolescence is an age where you feel out of place and where life is just a giant question mark. In my autobiography *The First Time I was 16,* I wrote: "I feel that life is always on the brink of begin- ning, but it never does! Mum, you always say I have a brilliant future ahead, so tell me, when does the future begin?"

I should never have turned the page!

Reality:

Ha ha, let's give that face a few more spots!

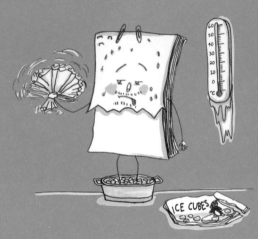

Write about problems or a difficult experience.

In the end, did it teach you something about yourself or other people?

"Problems are messages."
Shakti Gawain

Listen, gaze out, and think about the sea beyond the horizon. Where does it take your imagination?

"I must go down to the sea again, to the lonely sea and the sky,
And all I ask is a tall ship and a star to steer her by;
And the wheel's kick and the wind's song and the white sail's shaking,
And a gray mist on the sea's face, and a gray dawn breaking."
John Masefield

Do you think you will get married?

What will your wedding day be like?

"The world has grown suspicious of anything that looks like a happily married life."
Oscar Wilde

Invent your own National Anthem!

"Oh, say can you see by the dawn's early light
What so proudly we hailed at the twilight's last gleaming?
Whose broad stripes and bright stars through the perilous fight,
O'er the ramparts we watched were so gallantly streaming?
And the rocket's red glare, the bombs bursting in air,
Gave proof through the night that our flag was still there.
Oh, say does that star-spangled banner yet wave
O'er the land of the free and the home of the brave?"

Francis Scott Key

Write about your boyfriend or girlfriend.

If you don't have one, write
about the one you'd like to have!

*"Love is the difficult realization that something
other than oneself is real."*

Iris Murdoch

Write a story in which the hero receives some very surprising news.

"To be surprised, to wonder, is to begin to understand."
José Ortega y Gasset

Spend the day thinking of everything you couldn't live without: friends, places, familiar objects, letters, etc.

It's true, without you I wouldn't exist!

"Writing and reading is to me synonymous with existence."
Gertrude Stein

"I observe, I feel, I think, I imagine."

Helen Keller

Spend your day doing just one of the things Helen Keller mentions.

Helen Keller,
who wrote this
quotation, is a
mystery to me.
I don't understand
how someone who
was blind and deaf
managed to grasp the
essence of life so deeply.
Her life is truly
inspiring.

You have decided to write a book.
What will it be about?

"And at some point I muse that I too would like to write a storybook full of secrets and mysteries, full of counts and orphan girls and enchanted thieves, starring a bride and groom named Fania and Zigmunt ..."

Isaac Bashevis Singer

Give your parents some work to do!

Ask them to write down
something that they'd like
to teach you about life.
They can use this whole page!

"My son, forget not my law; but let thine heart keep my commandments:
For length of days, and long life, and peace shall they add to thee."
The Bible, Proverbs 3:1–2

Any time, every day,
whenever you feel like it,
write your thoughts down in a secret little notebook.

"It's not a bad idea to get in the habit of writing down one's thoughts.
It saves one from having to bother anyone else with them."

Isabel Colegate

From now on, force yourself to write something every time you have a spare minute.

You have to keep
your writing in training
so you don't lose your
touch (or your mind)!
It's like playing
an instrument, doing
a sport, speaking a foreign
language, or even cooking.
I start every day of my life
by writing in my journal.
It's like doing exercises
or having breakfast.
I can't imagine a day
without writing . . . at
least while I'm still alive!

"The way you define yourself as a writer is that you write every time you have a free minute. If you didn't behave that way, you would never do anything."

John Irving

Close your eyes for a good
few minutes, long enough
to imagine that you are blind.
Then open them.

What do you see now?

*"The real voyage of discovery consists not in
seeking new landscapes, but in having new eyes."*
Marcel Proust

Go to the theater!

Try writing a scene of your own.

The center of theater in the United States is in New York City, on Broadway. Broadway is known for its lavish musicals and searing dramas. Over 10 million people buy tickets to Broadway shows every year!

"All the world's a stage,
And all the men and women merely players.
They have their exits and their entrances;
And one man in his time plays many parts ..."
William Shakespeare

Go into a park or garden and write down all the names you know for the trees and flowers.

"The earth must tell everything
In the interrogation by the rain and the sun,
All it knows: grass, cyclamens,
Other flowers; the grass dries up and thistles emerge."
Yehuda Amichai

Do some
housework:
Make a bed,
do some ironing,
tidy your room, etc.
Do it as skillfully
and as carefully
as you can.
Then, write about it.

"We are not artists, we do the best we can."
Balinese proverb

Read the paper and choose a short article
from the local news page. Write it again,
keeping the facts but bringing in new details.

*"Let us take things as we find them: let us not attempt to distort them into what
they are not. We cannot make facts. All our wishing cannot change them. We must
use them."*

John Henry Cardinal Newman

So what is love for you?

Shakespeare
tells us that love
is mostly made
of sighs.
Snoopy from
Peanuts has
another definition:
"Love is a warm
blanket in winter
and vanilla
ice cream
with chocolate
sauce in summer."

Slightly damp,
but worth every
squeeze!

"Love is a smoke raised with the fume of sighs."
William Shakespeare

I'm on my way!

According to the Kabbala, a branch of Jewish thought, the world is fragmented into hundreds of pieces. But if we act with honesty and integrity, we can repair it.

What would be your priority if you wanted to "repair" the world?

"By receiving light and transmitting it, we repair the world."

The Kabbala

Don't tell your parents,
but spend the whole night writing down your hopes
dreams, and all your innermost wishes.

"If you want your dreams to come true, don't sleep."
Yiddish proverb

What would your "house of happiness" be like?

Describe it in as much detail as possible, or draw it!

"If we built the house of happiness, the biggest room would be the waiting room."
Jules Renard

Imagine how this story continues . . . and write the rest!

It was hot, boiling hot, and very humid.
I already knew it was going to be a very long day . . .

ICE CUBES

"And in the midst of winter, I found within me an invincible summer."
Albert Camus

Why do you absolutely not want to die?

Give at least five reasons.

"I don't want to die. I love my wife, my kids, my afternoon walks by the lake. I also love to write..."

Stephen King

Today invite a few friends for a "word party."

Pick any subject. Each player should write as many words as possible on this subject during a given time. When the time is up, let everyone read out loud his or her list in turn. Notice the different ways people think about the same subject.

"There are enough words for everybody."
Charles Bukowski

Use an advertising slogan
as inspiration
for an incredible story!

"He thought he saw a buffalo upon the chimney piece.
He looked again and saw it was his sister's husband's niece.
'Unless you leave this house,' he said, 'I'll send for the police.'"

Lewis Carroll

Proust realized that we have to face up to painful
memories—but we generally try to forget them.
We call it having a "selective memory."

Search in your
memory
for something
you would
rather forget,
and look
it in the face—
you may see it
differently.

Dare
I look?

"There is no one, no matter how wise he is, who has not in his youth said things
or done things that are so unpleasant to recall in later life that he would
expunge them entirely from his memory if that were possible."

Marcel Proust

Make a list of the funniest words you know.

Do the same with words that make you cry.

*"Words that weep,
and tears that speak."*
Abraham Cowley

Tonight, take time out to watch the sunset.

Then read stories about grandfathers, like
My Grandfather's Blessings
by Rachel Naomi Remen and
How to Be a Grandfather by Victor Hugo.

"The old man watched the sun going down
While the sun watched the old man dying."
Victor Hugo

If sad memories are too painful, write about them! It'll make you feel better.

Stapler

"A happy memory is no longer happiness,
A sad memory is still painful."

Lord Byron

Think of someone you like very much— what details attract you to this person? Do the same with someone you dislike.

"Hatred, like love, feeds on the smallest details; it swallows anything."
Honoré de Balzac

Start a story
with the name of a town.

Use real street names,
shops, and landmarks and follow
where the writing leads you.

Why does it always have to rain in Gloucester?

*"Doctor Foster went to Gloucester
in a shower of rain."*
Nursery rhyme

August

"Our bodies are our gardens to which our wills are gardeners."
William Shakespeare

Can you think of something that you managed to do through sheer will power?

August 2nd

*"... one of the things we talked about was how some people,
even at a great age, persist in 'seeing' memory the way children
do—as a cupboard or a drawer or a box of treasures underneath
the bed, a box that gets full and has to be cleaned out every now
and then to make room for new treasures they collect."*

Jane Kramer

What is in your memory's "treasure chest"?

Make a list, and then write about
your most precious "treasure."

"Dreams were invented so we wouldn't get bored while we sleep."
Pierre Dac

Invent a cure for insomnia.

Here is mine:
Get up early in the morning.
Make the most of every minute
(no, every second!) of the day.
Move yourself.
Move heaven and earth.
Run up five hundred stairs twenty times.
Don't try to go to sleep before midnight.

"We first make our habits, and then our habits make us."
John Dryden

Today do something
that you have never done before!

Eat a dish you've never tried,
read an author you've never read,
listen to music you've never heard . . .

"We make a living by what we get.
We make a life by what we give."
Winston Churchill

Make a list of your friends.
Think of the ideal present for each of them,
then ask what they think.
Were you right?

"I write entirely to find out what I'm thinking, what I'm looking at, what I see and what it means. What I want and what I fear."

Joan Didion

These are some of the reasons I write:

- Because it is terribly important to me.
- Because I like the physical sensation of writing, as a skier loves to ski or a sailor loves the sea.
- Because I hope to be loved for what I write.
- Because I love reading.
- I write to enjoy myself.
- I write to see how far I can go.
- I write for the flash of inspiration that appears in the middle of a paragraph and lights up my day.
- Because I love books.
- Because I have to earn a living (at least it helps!).
- I write to make friends.
- I write to find answers to my questions.
- I write to keep in touch with life.

Writing is something I have always done and will continue doing . . . I can't help it!

And what about you?

*"We only see and understand others
according to our character and way of life."*
Rabbi Tsadok HaCohen of Lublin

Write a description of yourself and your best friend.

Are you alike?

What! We're not at all alike!

My best friend   **Me**

"Writing is hard work. A clear sentence is no accident. Very few sentences come out right the first time, or even the third time. Remember this as a consolation in moments of despair."
William Zinsser

Write a sentence and rework it
until it "smiles" at you.

The dog smiled at Mr. Paper in the only way he could

"Those who advance too quickly go backwards even faster."
Mencius

Working break!
Write a sentence as quickly as you can,
then write it backward!

August 10th

*"Little fly, thy summer's play
my thoughtless hand has brushed away . . ."*
William Blake

Write the life story
of a fly.

Inspiration's coming . . .
inspiration's coming . . .
inspiration's coming . . .

"I hear America singing, the varied carols I hear;
Those of mechanics—each one singing his, as it should be, blithe and
*   strong;*
The carpenter singing his, as he measures his plank or beam,
The mason singing his, as he makes ready for work, or leaves off work;
The boatman singing what belongs to him in his boat—the deckhand
*   singing on the steamboat deck;*
The shoemaker singing as he sits on his bench—the hatter singing as
*   he stands;*
The wood-cutter's song—the ploughboy's, on his way in the morning,
*   or at the noon intermission, or at sundown;*
The delicious singing of the mother—or of the young wife at work—or
*   of the girl sewing or washing   Each singing what belongs to her,*
*   and to none else;*
The day what belongs to the day—At night, the party of young fellows,
*   robust, friendly,*
Singing, with open mouths, their strong melodious songs."

Walt Whitman

When you are away,

what do you miss most about home?

And what do you enjoy most about other places?

I'll give it a try...

"In films, murders are always very clean. I show how difficult it is and what a messy thing it is to kill a man."

Alfred Hitchcock

Make up a new episode
for your favorite TV series.

Invent a character based on someone
you know. Include all their qualities:
the good and the not so good!

"The work of art which I do not make, none other will ever make it."
Simone Weil

Um . . . absolutely . . . I've never seen anything like it!

Group activity!

Tell the same story
to several people and ask
them to write it down.
Compare their versions!

"It is during the night that it is most glorious to believe in the light."

Edmond Rostand

You have been locked
into a building—a store,
a library, etc. at night.
What happens?

"Love's true dwelling is a secret hiding place."
Romain Gary

Invent a secret
hiding place where
a love story takes place.

"The secret of a good sermon is to have a good beginning and a good ending and have the two as close together as possible."
George Burns

You have five minutes airtime
on the radio.

Prepare a speech with a beginning and ending that make excellent impressions.

Ladies and Gentlemen,
Have a good night.

"EAT, v. To perform successively (and successfully)
the functions of mastication, humectation, and deglutition."

Ambrose Bierce

Is there a food you find repulsive?
Write a poem about it!

*"I wanted to see all and have all.
I lived too hastily."*

Charles Cros

Spend the day living as slowly as possible.

*"I tried to describe the world not as it is,
but as it is with myself in it,
which obviously does not simplify matters."*
Jean Giono

Write about something like a journalist, reporting only the facts.

Now, write about the same thing,
but add your opinions and your feelings.

"With one word all is saved, with one word all is lost."

André Breton

Write your favorite words on scraps of paper.

Put them in a good hiding place. You'll be surprised when you look at them later!

"Because a word, as you should know, is a living thing."
Victor Hugo

Choose just one word
from yesterday's activity
and use it to begin a story.

"We may know it by different terms—such as griping, grumbling, whining, or belly aching."

Dale A. Robbins

Spend the day complaining!

"When you depart from me sorrow abides, and happiness takes his leave."
William Shakespeare

August 23rd

Write the story of a summer romance.

What is your boyfriend or girlfriend like?
How did you meet?
Did you have to meet each other in secret?

"The trouble is we neglect football for education."
Groucho Marx

Write a story about sports and how they make you feel.

"If a man does not make new acquaintances as he advances through life, he will soon find himself left alone. A man should keep his friendships in constant repair."

Samuel Johnson

Write a poem
for a friend, beginning
each line with a letter
from his or her name—
in order, if possible.

August 26th

"In the sweat of thy face shalt thou eat bread."
The Bible, Genesis 3:19

What is the strangest profession you have ever heard of?

"Inspiration is wonderful when it happens, but the writer must develop an approach for the rest of the time . . . The wait is simply too long."
Leonard Bernstein

Put an ice cube in your mouth
and write until it melts!

*"If a thinker jumps into the water, he won't try to swim,
first he'll try to understand the water . . . And he'll drown."*
Henri Michaux

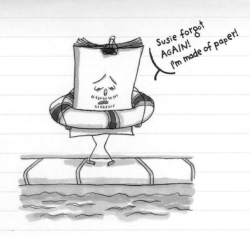

Invent the rules to a game,
and then play it with your friends.
Do your rules work?

"Style is the clothes that thoughts wear."
Philip Dormer Stanhope, Count of Chesterfield

Rewrite any of the quotations
in this diary in different styles.
Try writing in poetry,
or in the style of a famous author.
Be a journalist,
or rewrite a quotation
as a text message.

"The best menu is love."
Carlo Goldoni

Make up the menu for a romantic dinner.

"I think it is all a matter of love: the more you love a memory, the stronger and stranger it is."

Vladimir Nabokov

There we are, nice and cozy!

Your memories of summer are still fresh. Don't let the cold of winter drive them away.

Write about the summer memories you want to keep the whole winter through.

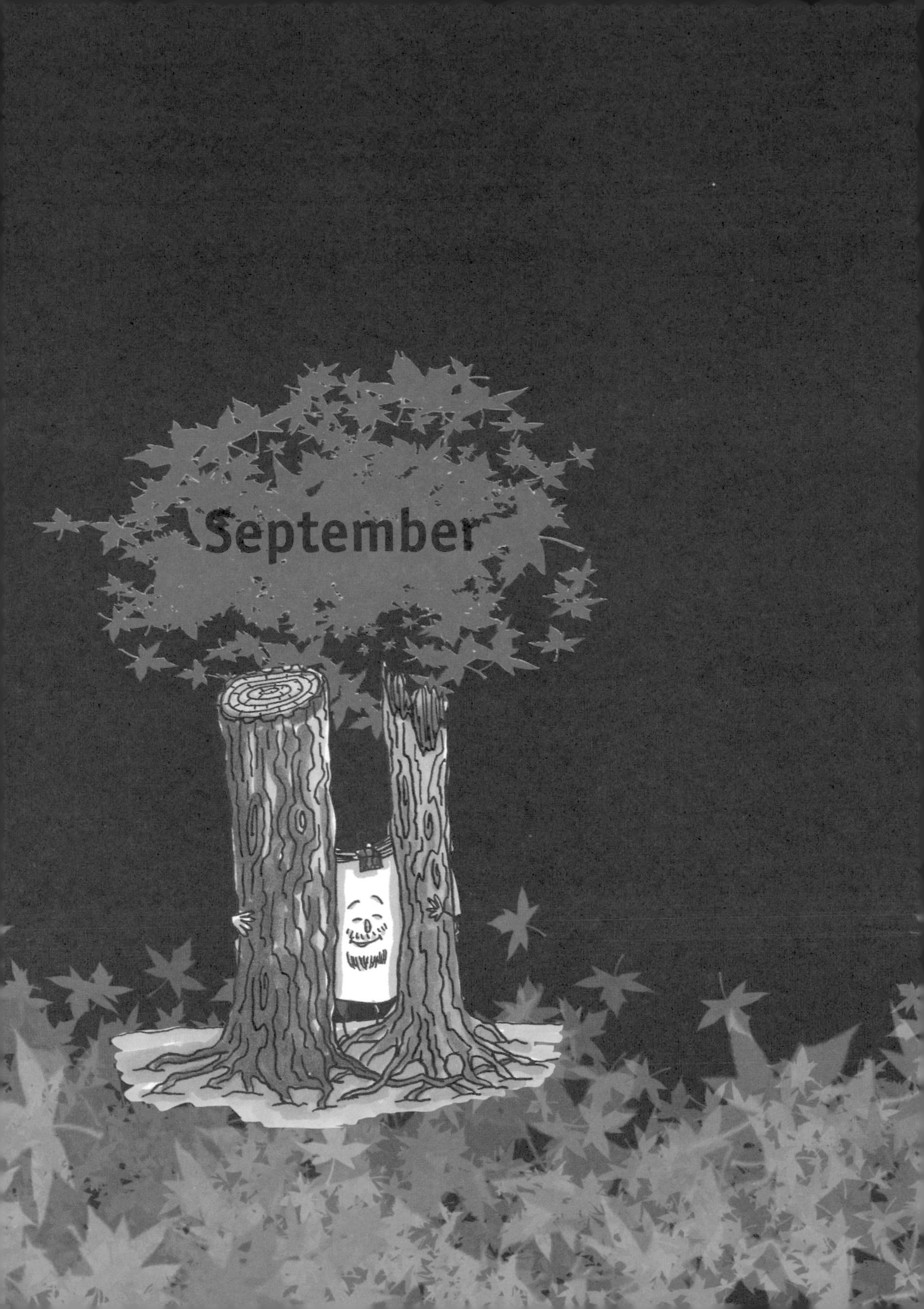
September

Write a message in code
on an ingeniously folded sheet of paper,
or on something unexpected
(a wrapper, a carton, etc.).

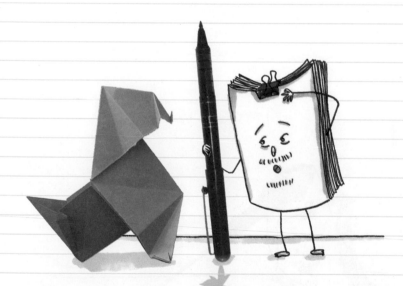

*"Let the important thing be how you look at things
and not what you are looking at."*
André Gide

"Even before I opened the letter, I knew what was in it."

Make up a story beginning
with this sentence.

very famous poet

"Nobody has ever measured, not even poets, how much the human heart can hold."
Zelda Fitzgerald

Do you remember the names of your classmates from two years ago?

Are you still friendly with any of them?

Ketchup with some old friends

"Friendship is the only cement that will ever hold the world together."
Woodrow Wilson

Every day this week
find the little things in your life
that make you happy, and write them down.

"To see a world in a grain of sand and a heaven in a wild flower;
hold infinity in the palm of your hand and eternity in an hour."
William Blake

Send a letter to someone who doesn't like you, or who doesn't accept you the way you are, and show them why they're wrong.

"A wise man gets more use from his enemies than a fool from his friends."
Baltasar Gracián

Write a list of ironic sentences like Dave Barry's.

The only meal . . .

The only nap . . .

The only music . . .

The only book . . .

"The only kind of seafood I trust is the fish stick,
a totally featureless fish that doesn't have eyeballs or fins."
Dave Barry

Think of a story where the hero (or heroine) acts against the majority!

September 7th

What inspired this reaction?
Could it be dangerous?

"Whenever you find yourself on the side of the majority, it's time to pause and reflect."
Mark Twain

Choose any subject
(night time, rain, shoes, etc.).

List all the words
you associate
with the subject
you have chosen,
and use them all
to write a poem.

HOLD ON!

- STOP!

ENOUGH
IS ENOUGH!

I CAN'T
SEE A THING!

*"Poetry is the confused reflection of our society
and each poet's breath clouds the mirror differently."*
Louis Aragon

Make up a story based
on your favorite song lyrics.

September 9th

*"You can dance, you can jive, having the time of your life;
See that girl, watch that scene, dig in the dancing queen."*
Abba

Write down a secret
in writing so tiny
that no one can read it!

Shh! I'll keep your secret.

"It's much easier to reveal one's true feelings to a diary
than to express them out loud! Oh how we flee reality!"
Bertrand Gauthier

Describe something ludicrous and totally imaginary about the start of the school year.

Something tells me this year is really going to be fun!

"Last night I had a crazy dream
That I was teachin' school.
My teachers had turned into kids,
And I laid down the rules . . ."
Shel Silverstein

Write a letter
to your parents,
thanking them
for something.

Thanks Mum,
thanks Dad!

"We should be grateful to our parents.
If they hadn't been tempted, we wouldn't be here."
The Talmud

What do you remember about nursery school and your first impressions of elementary school and middle school?

"And then the whining schoolboy,
with his satchel, and shining morning face,
creeping like snail unwillingly to school."
William Shakespeare

Empty out
your schoolbag
and describe
every object in it,
without saying
what it is.

"To name an object is to destroy three quarters of the joy of poetry, whose magic lies in revealing little by little: suggestion, that's what we dream of."
Stéphane Mallarmé

Remember to wash your hands!

Today
you've decided
to liven things up.
Tell the story . . .

"We travel comfortably along the motorway of life,
protected by the seatbelt of certainty and the airbag of routine."
Dave Barry

If you could design your school uniform, what would it look like?

Write down something you overhear in the street or on the bus, etc.

When you get home, imagine the rest of the conversation.

"We sometimes have conversations of such sadness that it seems all we have left is to consign ourselves to the grave."
Mme de Sévigné

Violence

What does this word mean to you?
Have you ever seen people behave
violently at home or elsewhere?

"Violence in the home is like a worm in fruit."
Yiddish proverb

Ask for a birthday present . . .

. . . from your best friend,
your mother, and your grandmother.
Change what you ask for
to suit the giver's age.

"Our birthdays are feathers in the broad wing of time."
John Paul Richter

What's the biggest fight you ever had with your mother?

"Sons whose mothers are still alive, remember that your mothers are not immortal. I will not have written in vain if one of you, after reading my death chant, is kinder to his mother, because of me and mine. Be kind to your mother every day. Love her better than I loved mine . . . No son really believes that his mother will die, and all sons get angry and impatient with their mothers. This folly is too soon punished."

Albert Cohen

What would your ideal life look like?

"To walk in fair weather through a fair landscape, in my own good time; and with a pleasant destination awaiting me: that, out of all the ways to live, is the nearest to my ideal."

Jean-Jacques Rousseau

Choose your father's
most annoying fault
and change places
with him. Today
you are the one
who has this fault . . .

All day you should think,
speak, and act in character.

"If you hate a person, you hate something in him that is part of your-self. What isn't part of ourselves doesn't disturb us."

Hermann Hesse

Do you think that human nature is basically good?

*"It's really a wonder that I haven't dropped all my ideals,
because they seem so absurd and impossible to carry out.
Yet I keep them, because in spite of everything
I still believe that people are really good at heart."*

Anne Frank

I think I'll stay here in bed and rest my paper-sleepyhead.

The main character in your book wakes up in the morning . . .

What is this character thinking about? Imagine what he's saying to himself.

"To wake up is to go in search of the world."
Alain

Today you are bored to death in class!

Escape from reality by inventing a story.
Begin like this:
"This classroom is not a classroom,
this teacher is not a teacher,
these students are not students."

Giddy-up, horsey! Giddy-up!

"I would say that, as a creator, the main part of my work consists of struggling against reality."

Jean Giono

Write a letter to one of your ancestors, someone you have never known but have heard about.

Introduce yourself and tell why you would have liked to have known him or her.

"Great-great-grandma's Bookbinders" at your service

Not yet, I'm not finished!

"What grape to keep its place in the sun, taught our ancestors to make wine?"
Cyril Connolly

Stare at the blank page in front of you and write about the first ghost that comes to mind!

"Writing is much like finding yourself in an empty house, and waiting for the ghosts to show up."

John Le Carré

Do you have an object
you like to talk to?
What do you talk about?

"Inanimate objects, have you then a soul
That joins with ours and lays claim to our love?"
Alphonse de Lamartine

What strikes you most about autumn?

Describe the smells, sounds, and colors of this time of year. Do you wear different clothes in autumn?

"Season of mists and mellow fruitfulness,
Close bosom-friend of the maturing sun;
Conspiring with him how to load and bless
With fruit the vines that round the thatch-eaves run;
To bend with apples the moss'd cottage-trees,
And fill all fruit with ripeness to the core."

John Keats

Continue this story:

"I'm totally broke!
When I think of all the things
I could get if I only had the money . . ."

Out of sight,
out of mind!

First of all I'd buy . . .

"Money is better than poverty, if only for financial reasons."
Woody Allen

October

Look around you
and "capture" ten words.
Imprison them in your head.

*"Words are
our slaves."*
Robert Desnos

Now, put them to work
all day long in your conversations.

So, whose turn is it next?

Are you haunted by regrets?

What's the matter?

Five years ago, I forgot to thank an eraser for removing a word.

"We give ourselves a lot of trouble inventing fears and regrets."

Alain

You are a journalist
for your school newspaper . . .

In the gossip column, write the gossip
going around about your friends.

"A secret is not
something talked
about, it's something
whispered in private
conversations."

Marcel Pagnol

"Love doesn't stand a chance without imagination."
Romain Gary

You are dressed like a ragbag, and you haven't washed your hair for a week.

That's just when you bump into the boy or girl of your dreams . . . Tell the story.

Imagine that you manage to do something impossible.

How do you go about it?
What do you use to help you?
What happens?
How do you feel?

"Man was created
to lift up the sky."
**Rabbi Menahem
Mendel of Kotzk**

Become an editor!

Your friend has written a novel.
Write a letter rejecting it, giving
details of what is wrong.

October 6th

*"You have to know
how to accept
rejection and
reject acceptance."*
Ray Bradbury

*"Walk on a rainbow trail;
walk on a trail of song,
and all about you will be
beauty. There is a way
out of every dark mist,
over a rainbow . . ."*

Virginia Woolf

Virginia Woolf was a British novelist and essayist (1882–1941).
She was one of the first feminists, and she dared to express her
thoughts and innermost feelings. I recommend reading *Orlando*,
The Waves, *To the Lighthouse*, and *Mrs. Dalloway*. If you want
to know more about her, you could see the film *The Hours*.
But I really suggest you read her books!

Go on and read them!

- Being born
- Living
- Being published

"*Man has but three events in his life:
    to be born,
    to live,
    and to die.
He is not conscious of his birth, he suffers at his death, and he forgets to live.*"

Jean de La Bruyère

Find three verbs that express the three most important stages of your life.

October 9th

"Ideals are like
stars: you will not
succeed in touching
them with your
hands, but like the
seafaring man on
the ocean desert of
waters, you choose
them as your guides,
and following them,
you reach your
destiny."

Carl Schurz

Didn't someone say
"The pen is mightier
than the sword"?

SHARPIE

What ideal would
you be prepared
to fight for?

One of your characters has an accident.

What happens to this person?
Does he escape unscathed?
Does anyone help?

"Gravity is a contributing factor in nearly 73 percent of all accidents involving falling objects."

Dave Barry

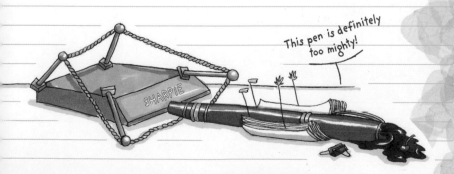

This pen is definitely too mighty!

Today, write a tourist brochure for your town.

"Man's real home is not a house but the Road and . . . life itself is a journey to be walked on foot."

Bruce Chatwin

Your brochure should contain a list of sights not to be missed . . . Include some personal favorites which may be off the beaten track. Illustrate with your own photos.

"Yesterday
is the past,
tomorrow
is the future,
but today
is a gift.
That's why
it's called
the present."

Bil Keane

I'm the king of the signposts!

The path of life ☆☆☆☆

Years gone by ☆

Write your horoscope for today.

"Who said life
was a dream?
Life is a game."
Jean Anouilh

Hey,
what are you
playing?

It's called
"Game of Chance."

If life were a game, what game would it be?

Write a dialogue where two people criticize an absent "friend."

October 15th

"One must be as ignorant as a schoolmaster to flatter oneself with thinking one has said a single word that has never been said before."

Alfred de Musset

Choose two words and put them together. Then write the definition of the word you have invented.

Yoohoo, anyone there?

What is your desk like?

Describe it, in as much detail as possible.

"If an untidy desk means an untidy mind, what can an empty desk mean?"

Anonymous

October 17th

Give fourteen reasons why you like reading.

I like reading because . . .

1.

2.

3.

4.

5.

6.

7.

8.

9.

10.

11.

12.

13.

14.

"A book is a window through which we can escape."
Julien Green

So, are you going to open up or not?

The Window to the World

Escape Edition

Oh no! I'm falling to pieces!

" . . . of making many books there is no end; and much study is a weariness of the flesh."

The Bible, Ecclesiastes 12:12

This quotation is the story of my life.
I spend most of my time sitting down, thinking up characters and situations, and I try to forget about my body.
But I have the feeling that I'm missing something by ignoring this part of myself.
I don't know how to meditate; I can't manage to empty my head of thoughts. I don't know how to wear out my body; I only know how to wear out my mind.
So whatever you do, don't be like me!

Lie down in a calm place and let your body do the talking.

> "I abhor the dull routine of existence. I crave for mental exaltation."
>
> **Arthur Conan Doyle**

Take a break from routine!

Today, add an unusual ingredient
to your everyday life.

Let it all out!

Write down everything you hate
about your math class.

This would be the best place for it . . .

"I know that two
and two make four—
and should be glad to
prove it too if I could—
though I must say if by
any sort of process
I could convert two
and two into five, it
would give me much
greater pleasure."

Lord Byron

October 21st

"Give me the splendid silent sun with all his beams full-dazzling."

Walt Whitman

What's the weather like? Write a story with the sun as the hero!

Stop sulking.
At least you're
not recycled!

500 sheets
80 g/m²

High quality paper

"We are all
jokers: we will
survive our
problems."
Emile Cioran

Invent a joke
about something
you find problematic.

There's an elephant in your school cafeteria.

What happens next?

"Writing a song
is like hunting.
You have to place
your instruments
like you place traps
to capture an animal
in the forest."

Björk

Write an article for your favorite magazine, then send it to the editor. You never know . . .

"There always comes a time when you have to choose between thinking and acting. It's called growing up."

Albert Camus

Make up an advertising slogan for your favorite chocolate.

Don't forget, your slogan must have punch and be catchy, so people remember it.

"Nothing is more dangerous than an idea when it's the only one you have!"

Alain

In your opinion, what would be the ideal way to die?

"There is nothing
ridiculous about
dying in the street
if one doesn't do it
on purpose."
Stendhal

You have a private meeting with the President.

Try to convince him of your point of view about the way the world is run.

"The pen is more
deadly than an
arrow."

Anonymous

Write an assortment
of curses for your enemies!

For example:
"May all your teeth fall out except one,
and may that one give you toothache!"

October 29th

"Fear is the father of hate."

Yiddish proverb

Have you ever been afraid of someone?

I think that hatred is based on fear.
We are all afraid of what we don't know.
In your opinion, were you right to be afraid?
Did you manage to get over your fear?
What made you change your mind?

"Heroes don't
smell very nice!"
Gustave Flaubert

Flaubert is telling us that the characters we create
do not possess only good qualities. In real life, people
are what they are—with all their good and bad points.
When you write a novel, you have to portray your hero
with all his imperfections.

Make up a story
about someone who
is a failure.

> "By believing
> passionately
> in something
> that still does
> not exist, we
> create it."
>
> **Franz Kafka**

Write a ghost story.

Here are the ingredients:
A haunted house, a brewing storm, and
an animal with a blood-curdling cry,
such as an owl or a wolf.

November 1st

"No sun—no moon! No morn—no noon—
No dawn—no dusk—no proper time of day.
No warmth, no cheerfulness, no healthful ease,
No comfortable feel in any member—
No shade, no shine, no butterflies, no bees,
No fruits, no flowers, no leaves, no birds,
November!"

Thomas Hood

Can you think of any more "no"s for November?

What do you like about November?

"Mathematics may be defined as the subject in which we never know what we are talking about, nor whether what we are saying is true."
Bertrand Russell

What if you wrote about a complicated subject of which you know nothing?

"Brilliant! I'll write about light bulbs!"

You can say absolutely anything, as long as you sound as if you know what you are talking about!

"A kiss is the only truly international language."
Alfred de Musset

Write about your first kiss, either how it was . . . or how you would like it to be!

"Every murderer is probably somebody's old friend."
Agatha Christie

November 4th

Your story begins with
the discovery of a corpse!

Give at least one clue
that will get your reader
hooked, and have him try
to guess who did it!

"I awoke one morning and found myself famous."
from Moore's *Life of Byron*

**Imagine you are
a famous celebrity
and write about
a day in your life.**

I'm a star!

"You become responsible, forever, for what you have tamed."

Antoine de Saint-Exupéry

If you planted
a handful of magic
seeds, what magic
powers would
their fruit have?

"When I think of all the books I have not read,
I know I still have happiness in store."

Jules Renard

You are an author.
Autograph your book
to a reader, signing
with a personal message.

I couldn't live without . . .

I couldn't live without . . .

I couldn't live without . . .

I couldn't live without . . .

I couldn't live without . . .

I couldn't live without . . .

What are your strong points?

What are your weak points?

Ask your friends, parents,
and other family members
what they think.

"A child's untidy room contains the building blocks of life."
Daniel Pennac

Your clothes have come to life!

What do they think about?
What do they eat?
Do they have any friends?
What about enemies?

A fight breaks out on your school playground!

Observe how each individual reacts.

> "Poetry and progress are like two ambitious men who hate one another with an instinctive hatred, and when they meet upon the same road, one of them has to give place."
> **Charles Baudelaire**

It's the year 2050 . . .

Where do people live?
How do they travel?
Do apples still grow on trees?

November 13th

"The superstitious will tell you never to walk under a ladder, but they won't stop you from walking under a taxi!"

Pierre Dac

Even if today isn't Friday the thirteenth, make a talisman to ward off bad luck.

"One, a robot may not injure a human being, or through inaction, allow a human being to come to harm; Two, a robot must obey the orders given it by human beings except where such orders would conflict with the First Law; Three, a robot must protect its own existence as long as such protection does not conflict with the First or Second Laws."

Isaac Asimov

November 14th

Imagine you are a robot!

Write your instruction booklet.

CLICK... CLICK... CLICK...

"Undoubtedly the desire for food has been, and still is, one of the main causes of great political events."

Bertrand Russell

There's a revolution in the school cafeteria.

What caused it?
Did you take part?

"Do not be too timid and squeamish about your actions. All life is an experiment."

Ralph Waldo Emerson

November 16th

Today at school talk to someone you'd like to get to know better.

We only have one life,
so live it to the fullest.
Living means talking,
sharing, taking action.
Life is a huge experiment.
So . . . let's try it out!

Take that, shyness!

Create a superhero and put him or her into a horribly sad adventure.

*"Praise would be worth a fortune
if it gave us the perfection we are praised for."*
Henry IV of France

You have just won the Nobel Prize in Literature!

Write the speech you are to give in two hours' time, in front of one hundred and fifty journalists!

"The worst lies are those one tells to oneself."
Marc Levy

Tell the story
of a compulsive
liar who finds
himself
or herself
in impossibly
ridiculous
situations.

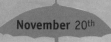

"Millions saw the apple fall, but Newton was the one who asked why."
Bernard Baruch

Imagine that you are free from the force of gravity and can fly!

November 21st

"The day we understand that animals can think without speaking, we will die of shame for locking them up in zoos and humiliating them with our laughter."

Boris Cyrulnik

Today your pet can speak!
What does it tell you?

OK, I let you out, and you teach me to swim!

*"A child of five would understand this.
Send someone to fetch a child of five."*
Groucho Marx

Is there something you do
better than your parents?

Write them a short explanation
of how to do it.

"It is fatal to be a man or woman pure and simple: one must be a woman manly, or a man womanly."
Virginia Woolf

Page for boys . . .

You are a boy.
Can you do
everything girls can?

My very own Prince Charming!

Girls . . . imagine what would be different in your life if you were born a boy.

They say that true intelligence lies
in anticipating what will happen . . .
but is that always possible?

Write a story
where nothing
happens as
expected.

"Writing: spending your time wrapping up a gift for a party that never happens."

Michel Polac

I'm just as good as a real book, you know!

Have a writing party!

One person writes a sentence. The second reads it and writes another.
Go round until everyone has written a sentence. Let the last player read the story!

"Happy the man, and happy he alone,
he who can call today his own . . ."
John Dryden

OK I'll wait . . .
but not for long!

Today . . .

What does the word "today" mean for you?

November 27th

"The crisis of yesterday is the joke of tomorrow."
H.G. Wells

Yesterday . . .

Remember how you wore that ridiculous pink ribbon?

Write "yesterday" at the top of the page, and jot down everything that comes into your head.

"Tomorrow to fresh woods, and pastures new."

John Milton

Write "tomorrow" and let the magic do its work on the whole page.

Tomorrow . . .

"Gather ye rosebuds while ye may,
Old time is still a-flying;
And this same flower that smiles today
Tomorrow will be dying."

Robert Herrick

Spend a day with
your grandparents.

Ask them about their best
memory and write down
the story they tell.

"I cannot tell how the truth may be;
I say the tale as 'twas said to me."
Sir Walter Scott

November 30th

Ask your grandmother to tell you a story that her grandmother told her.

December

"Papa, potatoes, poultry, prunes, and prism are all very good words for the lips . . ."
Charles Dickens

Write a list of ten words beginning with the same letter.

Now, write a story using them
in the same order as in your list.

OK, so who's the wise guy?

Paper

Words beginning with P

"It's statistically impossible for a girl of sixteen to unplug her telephone."

Daniel Attias

Telephone a friend to give some absolutely unbelievable news.

Wow!!

"In Xanadu did Kubla Khan a stately pleasure dome decree;
Where Alph the sacred river ran
Through caverns measureless to man
Down to a sunless sea."

Samuel Taylor Coleridge

December 3rd

Where would you like to live?

Imagine that you live
in an extraordinary place:
in a shell, in a tree, or on a boat . . .

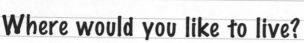

"A subject for a great poet would be God's boredom after the seventh day of creation."

Friedrich Nietzsche

You are bored to death.

Why? Where are you? Who are you with?

Don't worry, I've only been waiting for fifty years . . .

Editor

Waiting room

" 'I saw a Heffalump today, Piglet.'
'What was it doing?' asked Piglet.
'Just lumping along,' said Christopher Robin.
'I don't think it saw me.'
'I saw one once,' said Piglet.
'At least, I think I did,' he said.
'Only perhaps it wasn't.' "

A.A. Milne

December 5th

Invent an imaginary animal
(a girapotamus,
a bullephant . . .)
and describe it.

Thank you,
I'll be in touch,
Mr. Crocobook.

"My heart aches, and a drowsy numbness pains
My sense, as though of hemlock I had drunk,
Or emptied some dull opiate to the drains
One minute past, and Lethe-wards had sunk."

John Keats

One of your friends
is feeling miserable.
Send a letter to cheer
him or her up.

A singing letter for
the best manuscript
in the world · · ·

Reject

Priority

"Would you like to swing on a star,
Carry moonbeams home in a jar,
And be better off than you are,
Or would you rather be a pig?"

Johnny Burke
(song, "Swinging on a Star")

December 7th

It may be a little early, but you can still write to Santa Claus, or to your guardian angel, asking him or her to grant your special wishes.

"Nothing makes us grow as fast as a pair of stilts."
Professor Choron

Tell the story of a sock that lost its "significant other."

How does it react?
Is it completely lost?
What will become of it?

Dear
Mr. Paper,
Please come
and see me.
The Editor

"The creative act lasts but a brief moment, a lightning instant of give-and-take, just long enough for you to level the camera and to trap the fleeting prey in your little box."

Henri Cartier-Bresson

**Choose a photo
and write down
the memories
it brings back.**

Zoom on the signature

Contract for Mr. Paper to become a real book

The Publisher Mr. Paper

December 10th

Can you remember an occasion when you were very polite, though you would have preferred not to be?

"If I were to be given the opportunity to present a gift to the next generation, it would be the ability for each individual to learn to laugh at himself."

Charles M. Schulz

You receive a gift that you find odd: a bunch of hyacinths, a book of love poems, or a flashy shirt.

How do you react?
Are you very surprised or very angry?

Thanks, but I was kind of thinking of a book cover . . .

"One's friends are that part of the human race with which one can be human."

George Santayana

Make a list of everything you'd like to do with your best friend!

It's good to have a real friend!

Thanks for the trousers.

December 13th

"To see, to hear, to love. Life is a gift which I unwrap on waking every morning."
Christian Bobin

A genie presents you with a new life . . .

Where would you like to be born? What sort of parents would you have? Would you have brothers and sisters? Tell the story . . .

"Don't write naughty words on walls if you can't spell."
Tom Lehrer

If you were allowed to put graffiti on the wall at school, what would you write?

I AM HAPPY

"Men are born and remain free and equal in rights."
Declaration of the Rights of Man, 1789

December 15th

What does freedom mean for you?

"One good anecdote is worth a volume of biography."

William Ellery Channing

Write an anecdote about someone, famous or not, who struck you during this year.

"Fairies do their washing in a soap bubble, and cook by a fire of phosphorescence."

Béatrix Beck

You know anything about soap?

Sorry, only soup.

100 recipes Soup

Soap!

Invent a story about someone who is imprisoned inside a soap bubble!

"He who sings scares away his woes."
Cervantes

Invent a story where the plot doesn't go anywhere!

Your character is in exactly the same situation and in the same place at the beginning and at the end of the story, but he's tried at least three times to get somewhere.

"Procrastination is my sin.
It brings me naught but sorrow.
I know that I should stop it.
In fact, I will — tomorrow!"
Gloria Pitzer

December 19th

What kinds of things
do you always
put off doing?

Oh, my goodness:
I really have to start
my diet tomorrow!

Make a list,
then do them all!

December 20th

*"Twixt the optimist and the pessimist, the difference is droll.
The optimist sees the doughnut; the pessimist the hole!"*

Wilson McLandburgh

Make a pessimist's list about the past year.

Now make an optimist's list.

*"What's in a name? That which we call a rose
By any other name would smell as sweet. "*
William Shakespeare

I never thought I'd find a Red Thorneralia.

Tell the tragic story of a rose that has been picked and longs to return to her garden . . .

December 22nd

I want my cover!

Winter has begun. Your character is freezing cold. Write his or her icy thoughts.

"Somewhere, everywhere, now hidden, now apparent in what ever is written down, is the form of a human being. If we seek to know him, are we idly occupied?"

Virginia Woolf

Think about the main characters in your first novel.

What are their names?
How old are they?
What do they look like?
What do they do?
Do any of them have a burning passion?
How do they dress?
Do they have cars?
What are their short-term plans?
What do they want to do with their lives?
Where do they live?
What are their rooms like?
Who are they friends with?
What do they like to eat?
What are they good at?
What do they read?
What are their parents like?
Do they have brothers and sisters?

This is the story of my life.

December 24th

Tonight is Christmas Eve . . .

Whether you celebrate Christmas, Chanukah, Kwanzaa, or another holiday, write about your favorite family gathering. Give details!

"And unextinguish'd laughter shakes the skies."

Homer

Today is a holiday!

Whether it's your holiday or not,
eat, drink, and be merry all day long!

I must be dreaming!

December 26th

Choose something that you've written and send it to ten people.

Now wait for the mailman to
bring their comments. Be patient!

*"I keep six honest serving-men
(They taught me all I knew);
Their names are What and Why and When
And How and Where and Who."*
Rudyard Kipling

December 27th

Here are some of the questions that people ask me most often.

What do you think of when you are writing a book?
Why do you write?
When did you begin your first novel?
Where do you like to be when you write?
How do you get ideas?
Who is your favorite author?

What about you?

December 28th

Write a list of blunders you have made!

"Books aren't written—they're rewritten. Including your own. It is one of the hardest things to accept, especially after the seventh rewrite hasn't quite done it."
Michael Crichton

Invent the titles of
your future best-sellers.

So, what's your name?

Errm, I've changed it so often I've forgotten!

The Invincible BEST-SELLER

"Writing a book is an adventure. To begin with, it is a toy and an amusement; then it becomes a mistress, and then it becomes a master, and then a tyrant. The last phase is that just as you are about to be reconciled to your servitude, you kill the monster, and fling him out to the public."

Winston Churchill

Your pen refuses to write what you want!

So let it write what it wants!

"If you wish to be a writer, write!"
Epictetus

On your mark . . .

Get set . . .

Go!

This is where your novel begins!

The Aspiring Writer's Journal